BRIGHT YELLOW SUNSHINE

Cheyenne Bluett

Cover design by: Cheyenne Bluett
Illustrations by: Ashlyn Dunn
Printed in the United States of America

DEDICATION

This book is dedicated to all the people who forced me to grow -
whether thanks to love, pain, or indifference. Thank you for giving me a voice to help others like me.

To the reader:

My hope for you
is that while you read
these poems and prose
of self-love and sunshine,
you are filled with
a new fire of passion
and hope for yourself
to finally become
who you were meant to be
and love yourself entirely.

xoxo

You are not

the bad things

they have told you

or called you.

JELLYFISH

Jellyfish don't worry

about what is going to happen next,

they simply go with the flow and find out.

They float

and drift

and glide

and swirl through the water.

Don't let your anxiety crash into you like the waves.

When things are out of your control, go with the flow.

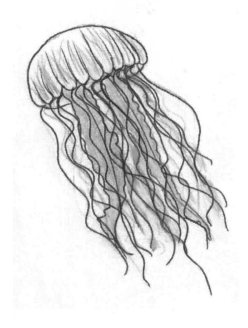

Her aura is
sunshine yellow
and
bubblegum pink

and

she does
what she wants,
not caring what they think.

Even though I know
you'll never be proud of me,

I am damn proud of who I am.

~ I don't need your validation anymore. I am enough for both of us.

I LOVE YOU, CELLULITE

Stretch marks,
belly fat,
off-white teeth,
I love you.

Body hair,
wrinkles,
and hip dips,
I love you too.

I want you to love the parts of you
that magazines don't want you to.

And then you'll see
how fulfilling it is
to love
every inch of yourself.

Maybe the reason
they watch you so intently
is because you make them believe
they can be happy too.

You are enough.
Good enough,
pretty enough,
smart enough.

You are more than enough
for anything you want to be.

Repeat and repeat again
until you finally believe it.

Stay because of
rainy days curled up on the couch
reading your favorite book and sipping coffee.

Stay because of
ice cream sundaes and crispy French fries
and Friday night date nights with friends.

Stay because of
your favorite song coming on the radio
as you drive home and you sing your heart out.

Stay because
we love you so much
and if you were to go,
we would never be the same.

I'm not the girl I was before;
I shed her like a snake skin.
The weak woman
who begged for a man's love,
who worked for others' validation,
who didn't love herself
is no longer here.

~   *It's never too late to shed your old skin*
        and be who you were meant to be.

You are worth

all the good things.

This big,
bright,
beautiful world...

needs you!

People always say that
your smile lights up a room,
but, sweetheart, it's not just your smile...

It's the musical sound of your laugh,
it's the graceful spring in your step,
it's the warm sunshine seeping out of your soul.

It's entirely you.

My all-time favorite
thing to do is
accomplishing the things
they said I could not.

Raspberry wine,
feelin' fine,
warm sunshine...
I love summertime!

Why do we try so hard
to be better than the other?

Can you imagine
what would happen
if instead,
we lifted each other up
and gave each other some tips?

We would all be greater together.

I owe my life
to coffee and chai lattes
keeping me awake
and dreaming.

Every day is a new day.
The moment you see sunlight
peeking through your eyelids,
you should
wake up,
stretch,
spring out of bed
and smile
because it is a new day
to make your dreams come true.

Why do you care what they think?

Who cares what they say?

What do *you* think?

How do *you* feel?

       That is what really matters in your life.

This is your only life.

This is your one chance to do

what you want and follow your dreams.

So what if they laugh?

So what if they think you can't do it?

    Prove.

        Them.

           Wrong.

Show them you aren't a force to be reckoned with.

Show them you are going to do whatever you want to do

and no one can tell you otherwise,

no one can change your mind,

no one can bring you down.

I don't care how big your dream is

or how farfetched you think it is,

if it's something you really want,

then quit the whining and

believe in yourself.

Make it come true.

I don't care how hurt you were
or how many times you failed...
Keep.
Going.

Get your booty back up and finish that dream
until your legs are tired
and you don't know how much you can walk anymore,
until you conquer it and your dream comes true.
This is your only life.
Are you going to sit back and let it pass you by,
or are you going to show this world who you are
and what you can make happen?

I feel the best
in a floral sundress
and strappy heels
with a pink headband
and a big, bright smile.

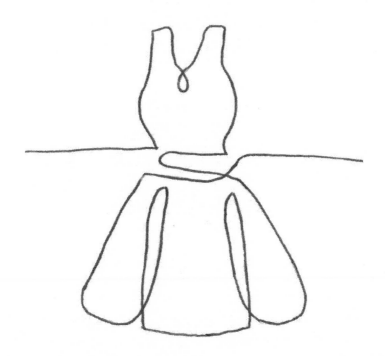

Always be a light.
You never know
who around you
has only been in darkness.

~ You can change the world one person at a time.

Every day
the sun rises
and shows us
how to start another day.

No matter how dark
last night may have been,
you can still rise
and shine
brighter than before.

Embrace who you are
and be her with *FIRE*.

Love yourself

with all the love you try

to give to everyone else,

and I promise you,

you'll never feel unloved again.

His Green Eyes may be beautiful,
but your big, bright smile
makes his eyes even more vibrant.

Without that smile,
his eyes wouldn't be
as bright,
sparkly,
or magical.

Don't forget
that, reflected in those eyes,
is your own beauty.

I pray you never

get tired of

loving yourself

completely and entirely.

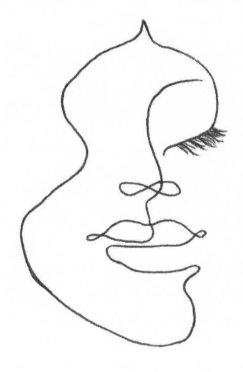

Everyone likes to laugh at the dreamers

until their dreams come true

and they are on cloud 9

while you are stuck in a 9 to 5.

~ Dream your heart out; it is worth it!

There is something so special
about staying up late
on a Saturday night,
surrounded by friends
and the smell of s'mores
and drunken giggles
because of whiskey.

It is never too late
to do what you want,
be who you want
or love who you want.

Be who you were meant to be
on the inside and out
starting now!

I am
completely,
entirely,
and absolutely enough
just the way I am.

And so are you.

You're not broken, sweetheart.

You've got your flaws like everyone else,

but I promise you,

you're going to be okay.

Toot your own horn.

Be proud of yourself.

Show off your goals and accomplishments.

You are an
amazing,
proficient,
one-of-a-kind
human.

End of story.

You could pick
the prettiest rose
and hold it up
right next to you...

and that rose
wouldn't even
stand a chance.

~ You are so extremely beautiful.

I will never conform myself
to fit in your tiny box
for I am wild, free,
and unapologetically me.

TO YOU AND TO MYSELF

I just want
to love you so good
that you will never
feel unloved again.

And one day,
I just woke up
and decided
I was going to do
whatever the *f*ck* I wanted.

You could confidently tell your friends

over and over again

how loved

    and brilliant

        and creative

            and kind

                and special they are...

but why can't

you even

whisper the words to the mirror?

For a very long time,

I always worried about making others happy

instead of myself.

I would focus on everyone else,

making sure no one was ever mad at me.

I put myself on the backburner

and wondered why I was never fulfilled.

Now I look back and see

all the wasted time

caring for people who

turned out to be the wrong people.

I finally realize that the one person

I can truly count on

and who I should make happy

is myself...

and ever since I've changed my ways,

my cup is always overflowing.

HELLO SUNSHINE

The sun speaks to me
and I bask in her warm embrace
feeling her power radiate through me,
feeling the ground beneath my feet.

I call on her
to energize me,
renew me,
and strengthen me.

Even when
I refused to love myself,
my heart never gave up.
She always kept beating,
knowing one day
I would.

And that day, my heart beat just the same.
But I know we were both
forever changed.

~   *I finally love myself.*

Remember through the storms,
the tornadoes, the hurricanes,
and the rain,
that the sun will always shine again.

If you want to be a dreamer
and conquer all of your wildest fantasies,
do not surround yourself with people
who never even shut their eyes,
for they will never understand,
and you will be left feeling alone.

Instead,
surround yourself
with those
who have an even bigger imagination
than yours—
and you will never feel alone again.

~   *Something I had to learn on my own.*

I don't know why I have to tell you
this same thing so many times,
but here I go again...

Stop

comparing

yourself

to

others.

Stop comparing

your life,

your looks,

your friends,

your experiences...

Stop comparing everything!

Do you want to know why you are different?
Because you are
supposed to be.
You were not created to be like everyone else.
I don't care if she looks perfect in your eyes.
You look perfect in my eyes
and you need to look in that mirror
and realize that yourself.

You must forget how amazing it is to be unique.
The definition of unique goes something like this:

Being the only one of its kind;
unlike anything else.

WOW.

Why does that not *inspire* you?
Don't you want to be who you truly are?
Don't worry about who they are.
There is only one you...
There ever will be only ONE. YOU.
And that is the greatest thing.

So please, stop trying to suck in your belly
or pose a certain way so you look a certain way.
Please stop trying to wear clothes
that make you feel uncomfortable
just because everyone else is wearing them.
Please stop trying to do things that you hate to fit in.
Please, stop trying to hide the real you.

Be who you are.
Embrace it with love and happiness.
Wear the clothes you love,
do your hair how you want,
eat whatever the hell you want
and make sure to take care of yourself after
(whether that be going to the gym or taking a nap).

Love yourself
and who you are—
differences and all
because you are most beautiful
when you let go
of who you think you're supposed to be
and are who you truly are.

~   *things I remind myself daily.*

The first time
I ever doubted myself
was the day you told me
I wasn't worth loving.

After you said that,
I realized *you* weren't.

And I never doubted myself again.

SCISSORS

For a really long time,
I would use scissors.
And if you know what that means,
then you used them too.

Put.
Them.
Down.

Stop using them.
Put them away
lock the drawer
and kiss those scars on your wrists.
Kiss those scars on your thighs and tummy too,
and whisper: Never again.
Your body is a temple.
Your body is love and your home.
Please, no more scissors.

Your body is worth kisses,
kind words, snuggles,
and love.

Start giving that to your body
and I promise your life will change for the better,
and your body and mind will thank you forever.

I know some days you wish it would all just stop.

I know that knowing it can never be cured
makes it even worse.

But if you work at it, it will get better.

You'll go from having panic attacks once a day
to once a week.
And then that'll turn to once a month, once a year,
once every few years.

Yes, I know it will never fully be okay.
It will never fully go away.
But you will always be able to improve
and you won't be so tired anymore.

Yay! You did it. Wow!

You got out of bed today!

You will crush this day.

Do not waste your time

begging for time

from someone

who doesn't even own a clock.

BURN BRIGHTER

Why do you care so much
about what other people think?
You have one life to do
the things that fuel your fire.
If they try to dull your flames,
burn brighter.

Never lessen who you are
in order to make
the wrong person like you.
The right people will love
all of you and more.

Embrace who you are
and embrace your differences...
Those are the best parts of you!
~ love yourself ~

Being called a woman
is one of the most powerful words
that is used to describe me.

SCARS

I have many different scars
due to many different things.
Some are from silly accidents,
others are from trying new things...

And some I made on purpose.

Don't be sad for me,
because I can happily say
that I haven't made any new scars
on purpose
for five years and counting.
I am so thankful for those scars,
because they remind me
where I used to be
and remind me
how much I have grown since then.

I am thankful for my new love for life,
I am thankful for overcoming even my darkest days,
and I am so thankful
that I choose to see that
in those scars today.

I know you think you won't get through this,
but I promise you:

You will.

You have survived each day
up until this point,
and you will continue
breathing,
beating,
and living.

I'm not saying it will be easy.
It won't.

Some days you will laugh until your belly aches.
Some days you will feel love like you never have.
Some days you will be tired.
Some days you will cry.
Some days, like today, will be hard.

You just must remember the good when all you see is bad.
You are stronger than the bad days.
You just need to believe it.

In your life,
your heart only beats a certain number of times.
No more, no less.
Once it stops, it stops.

What are you going to do
with each beat of life?

It's all up to you.

Growing up, I was told
to be a good woman
and to take care of myself
so that a man would fall in love with me.

I wish instead
I was told
to take care of myself,
nourish my dreams
and do what I please,
so I would fall in love with myself.

Do not ever let someone manipulate you
into feeling guilty
for not calling, texting,
writing a letter, driving to their house,
planning a date or making dinner
if they aren't doing so either.

Phones work both ways,
yet manipulation only takes one.

HARD TRUTHS

If you want to be in shape,
but you eat and cry on the couch,
you won't get toned.
If you want to love yourself,
but continue to bully your mind,
you won't fall in love.
If you want to be happier,
but don't leave your unhappy situations,
you won't feel better.

Change starts with *you*.
Are you going to just wish for a better life
or are you going to work for one?

~ I believe in you… Take the steps to believe in yourself, too.

Choosing to follow
the dreams inside of you
is scary.

No matter how grandiose,
exciting, fantastic,
and amazing they are,
deciding to give up your ordinary life
to be extraordinary
is terrifying.

But here's a secret:
You can do it.

Break the cycle of being 'normal.'
Embrace the fear
and conquer it
to become the exceptional,
rare, and unique person
that you truly are.

That's who we truly want to see.

Don't just love
the parts of yourself
that everyone else can see.
Love the parts they can't see
and the ones you try to hide,
because those are the pieces
that need your love the most.

Do not compare yourself
to someone else.
The snow is magnificent and cold
while the sun is stunning and bright.
The flowers are astonishing
in their own way, too.
But, darling, so are you.

LOVING YOURSELF IN EVERY COLOR

Love yourself
when you feel red.
Red is high heels with a black dress
and feeling sexy on a Friday night.
Or red is being angry
at someone who did you wrong.
The good, the bad,
the sexy, the angry...
Love yourself when you are red.

Love yourself
when you feel orange.
Orange is the rising sun at
6:30am in the morning
when you get ready for another day.
Or orange is the fallen leaf
that you crunch on as you walk
outside in October.
that you snack on while watching movies.
The good, the bad,
the hopeful, the changing...
Love yourself when you are orange.

Love yourself
when you feel yellow.
Yellow is daisies
that you pick for yourself just because.
Or yellow is the dress
with the polka dots
that makes you feel beautiful.
The good, the bad,
the gifts, the beautiful...
Love yourself when you are yellow.

LOVING YOURSELF IN EVERY COLOR

Love yourself
when you feel green.
Green is his eyes
when he leans down to kiss you
and make you feel so loved.
Or green is plants
that live in your home
that you tend to and help grow.
The good, the bad,
the love, the growth...
Love yourself when you are green.

LOVING YOURSELF IN EVERY COLOR

Love yourself
when you feel blue.
Blue is your irises
that sparkle when you're happy.
Or blue is tears that you cry
when the world seems to crumble around you.
The good, the bad,
the happy, the sad...
Love yourself when you are blue.

LOVING YOURSELF IN EVERY COLOR

Love yourself
when you feel violet.
Violet is the euphoria you feel
when you finally land your dream job.
Or violet
is the color of your own royalty.
The good, the bad,
the dreams, the queens and kings...
Love yourself when you are violet.

The good, the bad...
Love yourself
through all the
colorful parts of your life.

Dance like nobody's watching—
and if they do,
invite them to dance with you.

Live life freely,
but encourage others
to embrace it too.

I want you to know that
it's okay to cry.

Cry as much as you like.
Cry as much as you need to.
Cry until you're void of tears,
until all the sadness, pain,
negativity, and worry
are no longer in your body.

Shed the tears
and open your soul
to allow good things
to replace the bad.

This is your one life
to do what you want.
Don't let other people dictate
how you should feel,
what you should do
or who you should be.

Choose *you*,
and if they try to make you
feel guilty for doing so,
then they don't deserve to be
in your life anyway.

Do the things
that scare you most,
for those things will change you
in all the best ways.

Breathe in
4.
Breathe out
8.

Relax and refocus...

Breathe in
4.
Breathe out
8.

You are going to be okay.

Not everyone is going to like you,

and that is perfectly okay.

Their opinions don't matter anyway!

I do not need your validation
to **grow**.

I do not need your validation
to **thrive**.

I do not need your validation.
Period.

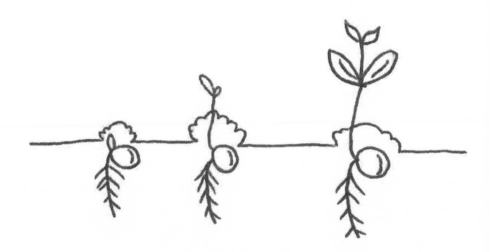

Goodnight, my love.
I hope you sleep safe and sound
as blankets envelope you in warmth
and cuddle your body softly.
When your head hits the pillow,
I hope you dream of life and love
and have the strength
to wake up again
and conquer tomorrow.

You make me want
to be a better person
in every way
and every pain
that I would rather ignore.

Sunshine,
oh, how I love you so.
Please shine on me eternally
and never let me go.

The day you were born

the angels sang the loudest they ever had,

the flowers bloomed bigger than ever,

the sun shined a million times brighter,

and all our lives changed for the better.

you were not
created by
accident.

you are here
for _so_ _many_
reasons!

Darling,
you belong among the stars,
not on earth like the rest of us.
You deserve your own constellation,
shining bright and dazzling.

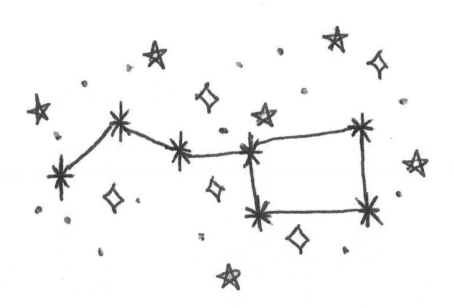

You have been and always will be enough, whether that's being smart enough, talented enough, pretty enough, etc. The most important person you can be enough for is yourself. Please remember this and say it daily. You. Are. Enough.

You have to take care of yourself before you can take care of others. If you constantly give and give and give, you will be left empty. You cannot pour from an empty cup. If you start giving yourself the love and attention that you give to everyone else, you won't even have to focus on giving yourself away, because you will be so happy that your cup will overflow into theirs. I promise you. Put yourself and your needs first and you will thrive.

You and your life matter. I don't need to elaborate. Just know
without a single doubt in this world that you matter.

Don't compare yourself to someone else. Everyone has different timelines in their life. You might be comparing your beginning to someone else's middle, so you are only making yourself feel worse! Regardless if you will get married at 18 or 45, finish your degree at 24 or 30, get your dream job at 26 or 37, your time will come when it comes. No matter if you believe in God, The Universe, Mother Nature, whatever, believe that your time will come when it is ready.

Follow your dreams. No matter how big, scary, silly, farfetched, or crazy they are. You CAN conquer your dreams. You CAN be the best version of yourself. Allow yourself to dream and then pursue that dream… because it will change your life for the better. You have one life - this is it. Don't you want to live this life for *you?!* Don't let your fear get in the way. Don't worry about what they will think, don't worry about if you will fail… just do it! Because *you can and you will!*

I believe in you. I love you. I am proud of you.

There is no one else
on this planet
exactly like you.

**AND MY GOODNESS
ISN'T THAT AMAZING!**

You're the only *you*
in this life,
in this whole wide world,
in this infinite universe.
Now that is something you should be proud of.

You are accepted and adorable,
brilliant and bright,
charming and cool,
daring and delightful.

You are enchanting and exquisite,
fun and friendly,
genuine and graceful,
handsome and heavenly.

You are independent and intuitive,
jubilant and joyous,
kind and knowledgeable,
lovely and luminous.

You are motivating and meaningful,
natural and nice,
optimistic and original,
powerful and peaceful.

You are a queen—
remarkable and refreshing,
special and spirited,
thriving and thrilling.

You are unbroken and unimaginable,
vibrant and victorious,
wholesome and witty,
and YES and zealous.

You are every good word.

I

will

not

change

who

I

am

in

order

for

you

to

love

me.

It's okay to be sad
sometimes,
but never forget
the *warrior*
that you are.

Yes, you are pretty.
But you are *so much more* than that.

You are a strong soul,
    a warm heart.
Soft arms that heal others with hugs.
Eyes that can either say
    I love you
or
    don't mess with me.
You are legs that walk to your destiny,
a voice that expresses yourself,
    and so much more...

Don't confine yourself to 'pretty'
when you are **extraordinary.**

Celebrate another person's wins,
even if you haven't finished yours yet.

Congratulate your competition,
even if they started off better than you.

Don't be bitter,
but full of love.
You can be both successful
and supportive
simultaneously.

When you left,
you took a part of me
with you.

I felt that pain
as long as I needed to.

But now I am rebuilding
that empty part of my soul
with love, joy, and peace
and I'm creating an even better version of me
that you will no longer
be able to touch.

HARD TRUTHS 2

A friendship built on
gossiping, complaining,
surface issues, and negativity
will never fulfill you.

No matter how much you may love them,
if they aren't helping you grow,
supporting you wholly,
or choosing to be by your side
through thick and thin,
then what are they in your life for?

Life is too short
for meaningless friendships.

Find people who
cheer you on, love you totally,
want you to succeed,
and stick with you through anything.

I promise they are out there.

Life won't always be sunshine and rainbows.

But it is up to you to choose
to remember that bright yellow sunshine
and let that guide you,
even when all you can see is clouds.

Groovy, Fly, Phat, Sweet,
Cool, Rockin', Dapper, Tubular.
Words of endearment may change
throughout the decades,
but in each one of them,
you've still stayed incredible.

Honey, eat the damn chocolate.

You are so much more beautiful
when you happily enjoy life
no matter your shape or size.

I forgive you.
Not necessarily because I want to,
but because I need to.

I forgive you
because it hurts me more
to hold on to the pain
that you caused me
than to just set you free.

And as of now,
you no longer have a hold over me.

Look in that mirror
and remind yourself
that you can do *anything.*

But, Cheyenne, how do you know that things will get better?

I'm glad you asked...

When I was sixteen years old, I was diagnosed with depression
and anxiety.
I had endured physical and emotional abuse as a child,
and I was also bullied as a child by my peers.
And when I was sixteen, it all came crashing down onto me.
I stopped eating.
I started self-harming.
I fell into a horrible depression, feeling hopeless and unworthy of
everything.

Then on December 13th, 2013, I tried to commit suicide.

Luckily, I was interrupted and taken to the Emergency Room,
where I spent the whole day crying until I was unable to produce
any more tears, and then I went to a Behavioral Health Center to
get the help I needed.

After six days in the Health Center, I was released and so happy to
be alive!

I want to say after that, I got better right away, but I didn't. I re-
lapsed, and on February 11, 2014, I tried and was caught again.

I remember being so hopeless in life that I thought: *I can't even kill
myself right!*

I ended up back in the Health Center—this time, 12 days in-pa-
tient and then 6 weeks outpatient.

And now, six years later, I wrote this book for *you*.

I can happily tell you that now I am one million times better. I have a love for life that I never thought I could have, I love myself and who I have become, and I am just taking life one day at a time.

Do I still have depression, anxiety, and trauma? Oh yeah. But I take medication, go to therapy twice a month, and have a huge support system in my family, husband, and close friends.

I still have days where I can't get out of bed. I still have days where I have panic attacks and struggle with why I am alive. I know that I will never be 100% cured of my disorders and pain, but I will never give up.

Every day, *I choose life.*

And that is what I hope this book reminds you what to do.

Life is hard. I know that. You know that.

But you can still choose to see the sunshine, even when there is a wall of clouds in the way.

I personally never thought I would still be here. And I am so thankful that I am.

When you think about giving up, dream! Dream about what your life would be like in 5 years, then 10 years, then 20 years. Will you have a pet? Be in school? Working your dream job? Loving yourself above anyone else? Get married? Start a business? Write a book? Your possibilities are endless!

I want you to remember this every single day:

- ♥ You are strong.
- ♥ You are enough.
- ♥ You are worth more than you could ever know.
- ♥ You are worth loving the life you live.
- ♥ You are worth *living a life you love.*

You are in charge of your life and you can make anything happen.
You will get through the bad parts.
You can *do this!!!*

No matter what people say and no matter how tired you may feel,

You. Can. Do. This.

I believe in you.

XOXO

ACKNOWLEDGEMENTS

Thank you to my wonderful husband, who, even on my worst days, encourages me to follow my heart and conquer my dreams. Thank you for believing in me more than I do myself sometimes!

Thank you to my supportive and loving family. You mean so much to me. I wouldn't be where I am today if it wasn't for you!

Thank you to my friends who not only still love me after hearing me talk about this book every day for the past few months, but also support me in every way, shape, and form!

Thank you to my Launch Team who helped get this book off to an amazing start!

And last, but not least, thank YOU! Thank you for taking the time to read my book. I truly hope you enjoyed it.

BOOKS BY THIS AUTHOR

His Green Eyes

"His Green Eyes" by Cheyenne Bluett takes the reader on a heart-felt journey of true love. Through soulful poetic storytelling, this poetess connects hopeful romantics to a type of love that knows no bounds. Page by page, each reader is given the opportunity to experience an awakening that reminds them that romance and chivalry are very much alive. By book's end, you will be left with a warmed heart, uplifted soul, and beaming face.

ABOUT THE AUTHOR

Cheyenne Bluett

 Cheyenne Bluett was born and raised in Springfield, IL. She has been writing since she could read. This is her second poetry novel and she is currently working on many more, as well as a YA Romance series! Besides writing, you can find Cheyenne crafting, baking, running a motivational blog off her Instagram, hanging out with her husband and fur babies, reading, or napping.

What's next?!
Follow her Instagram : @ thecheyennebluett

CAN YOU HELP?

Thank You For Reading My Book!

I really appreciate all of your feedback, and I
love hearing what you have to say.

I need your input to make the next version of
this book and my future books better.

Please leave me an honest review on Amazon letting
me know what you thought of the book.

Thank you so much!

xoxo,

Cheyenne

Made in the USA
Columbia, SC
18 November 2020